Nature's Children

COUGARS

Katherine Grier

Grolier

FACTS IN BRIEF

Classification of the cougar
    Class: *Mammalia* (mammals)
    Order: *Carnivora* (carnivores)
    Family: *Felidae* (cat family)
    Genus: *Felis*
    Species: *Felis concolor*

World distribution.   Exclusive to North America.

Habitat.   Mountains, swamps, forests, river valleys.

Distinctive physical characteristics.   Coat in varying shades of brown with black on the back of the ears, tip of the tail, and in stripes on the muzzle; white chest and throat.

Habits.   Solitary; most active at night; males mark territory with scent and by scratching with their claws.

Diet   Mainly deer and other fairly large mammals.

Published originally as
"Getting to Know . . . Nature's Children."

Canadian Cataloguing in Publication Data

Grier, Katherine
  Cougars

(Getting to know—nature's children)
Includes index.
ISBN 0-7172-1928-3

1. Pumas—Juvenile literature.
I. Title. II. Series.

QL737.C23G74 1985   j599.74'428   C85-098708-3

Contents

Sssssh! A cougar is coming! It prowls slowly,
silently through the deep, dark forest.
Suddenly it stops. It lets out a terrifying call
that sounds like a human scream. Then, quick
as a wink, it vanishes into the night.

Is it any wonder that the cougar has been
nicknamed "mountain devil" and "sneak
cat"? But you might be surprised to learn that
it has also been called "lord of the forest" and
the "greatest of wild animals." You would
almost think that people were talking about
two different animals, wouldn't you?

Just what is the truth about the cougar? Is it
a sneak or is it one of nature's nobility? The
only way to solve the mystery is to find out
the facts.

Puma, panther, painter, wildcat,
mountain lion—all these names are or
have been used for the same animal:
the cougar.

Soft Balls of Fur

As soon as her babies are born, a mother cougar holds each kitten with a huge but gentle paw and licks it clean and dry. Soon the kittens are snuggled up against her soft, furry belly, nursing on her rich milk. When they are full, they will fall asleep by her side, curled up together for warmth.

Before long, the kittens will be spending less time sleeping and more time playing and tussling in between naps. All this is great fun, but it is more than that. Playing helps the kittens build up their muscles and it helps teach them how to pounce and grab hold— valuable lessons for when they grow up.

Playful as a kitten.

All in the Family

The kittens and their mother make up one small family. But cougars are also part of a much larger family that spans the world—the cat family. Even though cougars are not small animals, zoologists place them in the "small" cat branch of this well-known family. Why? Simply because cougars cannot roar! They can only purr and yowl. The "big" cats, such as lions, tigers or jaguars, are just the opposite. They cannot purr—but do they roar! And then there are the cheetahs. They have a branch of the cat family all to themselves. They are the only cats that cannot pull in their claws!

The cougar's closest relatives in North and South America are also small cats. They are the lynx, bobcat and, believe it or not, the everyday ordinary house cat. You may ask "what about the mountain lion or puma"? Don't be fooled! These are just different names for the cougar.

Usually the cougar's lair is a small cave or crevice in the rocks.

Cougar Country

Cougars used to live in many parts of North America. How did the same animal manage to live in such different places as forests, prairies, lowlands, mountains, hot areas and cold? They managed because their needs are simple: all they need is food, such as deer and some smaller animals, a bit of cover from which to hunt and some slight shelter from cold weather.

Cougars could once find those things in all sorts of places. But as towns and farms spread over much of the land, cougar country shrank. Now most cougars in North America live in the mountains of the west.

*Where cougars
live in North
America.*

Keeping clean.

10

One Cougar Only!

Today a cougar's home is a piece of mountainland called its territory. Cougar territories are usually quite large compared to most animal territories. They must be large so that the cougar can find enough food.

Once a cougar has found a territory, it guards it carefully by making signs to tell other cougars "I live here." These signs are called scrapes. The cougar makes them by scraping leaves and dirt into heaps and mixing them with its urine or droppings. It also scratches trees in different parts of its territory and sprays them too. When other cougars see and smell one of these scratching posts or a scrape, they usually go the other way rather than risk a fight.

The cougar uses its claws to post "No Trespassing" signs.

Big and Powerful

The cougar is one of the biggest cats in all of North and South America. Only the jaguar is bigger. Not including the tail, an average-sized female is about one and a half metres (5 feet) long and weighs about 40 kilograms (90 pounds). The male is almost twice as large.

The cougar's long, muscled legs give it lots of leaping power. Because its back legs are slightly longer than its front legs, it always looks as if it is heading downhill, even when it is standing on flat ground. If you have ever watched a house cat jump, you will know that most of a cat's jumping power comes from its hind legs. It gathers its hind legs up under it and then springs forward. Thanks to the cougar's long, strong hind legs, it can leap as far as seven metres (23 feet) at one time. That is like jumping across a city street at a single bound!

To keep it balanced as it leaps, the cougar uses its thick, heavy tail as a rudder.

Sneaking up on Dinner

You might expect that a strong animal like the cougar would be a strong runner too. That is not the case. The cougar can run fast, but only for a very short distance. Because it tires quickly, it must rely on stealth to sneak up on its dinner.

How can an animal as big as a cougar avoid being seen as it stalks its prey? The cougar's tawny coloring helps it blend in with its surroundings so that it is difficult to see.

If you look closely you will see that a cougar does not have just one color of fur. It has patches of white and black fur just below its nose that look a bit like butterflies resting on its big upper lip. The back of its ears and the tip of its tail are black too.

If a cougar wants to let another animal know how it feels, it moves its ears and tail. The black markings draw attention to a switching tail or laid-back ears. But if a cougar does not want to be seen, it can keep very still and the darker patches blend in to the natural shadows of its environment.

Opposite page:

On the prowl.

Silent Paws, Sure Claws

The front and hind paw prints of the cougar look much the same because the thumb on the front paw is higher up and does not touch the ground when the animal walks.

Front

Hind

The cougar would not be able to move so quietly and steadily through its territory if it were not for its broad, heavy paws. There are four toes and a thumb on each front foot and four toes on each hind foot. A leathery pad on the bottom of each toe and at the base of each paw muffles the sound of the cougar's footsteps. And the cougar can spread its toes wide to grasp rough ground for extra traction.

On each toe, the cougar has a little pocket that holds a very sharp, curved claw. Each one is about as long as your big toe. When the cougar wants to move silently, it pulls its claws into these pockets. But when it wants to climb a tree or hold its prey, out pop the claws to give the cougar a good grip.

A lofty perch in a tree is an ideal spot to wait for passing game.

18

Super Sight

Like all animal hunters, the cougar must see its prey before the prey sees it. Very keen eyesight helps the cougar spot animals that are quite far off. And because the cougar pounces from a certain distance, it must know how far to leap. The cougar's eyes are placed in the front of its head and this helps it tell how far away things are.

Deer, the cougar's main prey, have good eyesight too. But they cannot judge distances as well as a cougar can because their eyes are more to the sides of their head. This is very helpful to a deer and other prey animals because it allows them to watch for hunters trying to sneak up from behind. No wonder the cougar must be such a stealthy hunter!

Like many animals, cougars are color blind. They see only in shades of black, white or gray. But they see much better at night than we do and so are excellent night hunters. This is especially important in summer, when the days are hot and most prey animals feed at night.

Opposite page:

If a cougar does not manage to catch its dinner at night, it will hunt on right through the day.

21

Deer for Dinner

Although the cougar's main food is deer, it hunts other animals too, such as moose, mountain goats, coyotes, bear cubs, porcupines, rabbits, birds and mice. One zoologist even tells of watching a cougar eat a whole meal of grasshoppers!

Ideally, a cougar needs to eat about four kilograms (9 pounds) of meat a day—about as much meat as there is in 36 hamburgers! That works out to one deer every seven to ten days.

It is easy to feel sorry for the cougar's prey, but in fact, the cougar is doing a very important job. In winter especially, it is difficult for a deer herd to find enough leaves, twigs and grass to eat. The cougar kills deer that are old, weak or sick, leaving more food for the strong, healthy deer. If the cougar did not kill the weaker deer, the whole herd would suffer and many might die of starvation.

When hunting, the cougar relies more on its eyes than its nose.

Let the Feast Begin!

Once a cougar has caught its prey, it usually likes to eat in a protected place. Often it will drag its catch to a favorite eating place or even carry it up to the branch of a tree.

When it comes to eating, the cougar is well equipped. It has special scissorlike teeth that cut the food into pieces small enough to swallow. This is important since the cougar does not chew its food first. And to ensure that not a morsel is wasted, the cougar's tongue is covered with short, sharp hooks to clean all the scraps from the bones.

A cougar cannot eat a whole deer in one meal. It hides what is left under leaves, branches or stones. If fresh food is hard to find, it will go back to this stored food many times. But if hunting is easy, it will leave its catch after only one meal. Cougar leftovers are not wasted. Other animals and birds eat anything the cougar leaves behind.

In a dry area such as this, a puddle of water provides a welcome drink.

Cold-Weather Cougars

The cougar does not prepare for winter the way some animals do. It does not gather up supplies of food as the chipmunk does or eat to put on fat and sleep away the winter months like the woodchuck. After all, the cougar's main prey, the deer, stays out all winter, so it can too. To keep warm as it hunts, its coat grows longer and thicker.

Actually the cougar's fur coat is two coats in one. Close to its body is a thick layer of inner fur. This holds in body heat and helps keep out the cold. A second layer of long guard hairs sheds snow and rain.

The cougar does not shed its coat all at once as some animals do. Hairs are lost and grow in all year long. In winter the cougar's coat is at its longest and thickest.

To find food, a cougar may travel up to 40 kilometres (25 miles) in a single day.

Hard Times, Good Times

If a winter is hard on the deer, it will be hard
for the cougar too. If there are not enough
deer, the cat must hunt smaller animals to
survive. They are just as hard to catch as deer,
and the cougar must catch more of them to
feed itself. And as the snow gets deeper,
hunting gets harder because the cougar is
heavy and sinks into the snow. Fortunately,
cougars do not have to eat every day. In fact,
they can go for days without a bite.

Although there are hard times for the
cougar, there are good times as well, when
prey is easy to find. After hunting, there is
little for the cougar to do but keep clean and
rest. The big cat licks itself all over and
sharpens its claws. Then it stretches out on a
favorite rock or drapes itself over the branches
of a favorite tree. There the cougar will spend
the day dozing or basking in the sun or simply
watching the world go by. However, if the
cougar is a female, she may also have the busy
task of raising a family to take up her
days . . . and nights.

Overleaf:
*The two-week
mating period is
the only time you
might see two
adult cougars
together.*

Opposite page:
*The cougar's
unusually long tail
sets it apart from
the other wild cats
of North
America.*

Courtship Calls

Cougars can mate any time of the year, but more often than not, they mate early in the winter. The female cougar leaves her home territory to look for a mate. She calls as she pads through new territories. Sometimes she meows like a house cat, only louder. And sometimes her voice rises in a scream that can be heard a long way away.

Finally a male cougar hears her calling or smells her scent. He sets out to find her. If another male is following her as well, they may fight to decide which of them will mate. Usually the strongest male wins.

The male and female cougars stay together for only about two weeks. Shortly after they have mated, the female travels back to her own territory to await the arrival of her new family.

Before her young are born, she searches for a den. She might choose a tangle of tree roots or a rocky cave as a nursery. There her kittens will be safe from enemies and bad weather.

Smitten with Kittens

Three months after the adults have mated, the kittens are born. There are usually two to four kittens in a litter—and they are helpless. Their eyes are tightly shut, and they can hardly crawl. But their mother is there to look after them. She tends to each one carefully, licking it clean with her scratchy tongue and then letting it nestle in close to her belly. Soon the babies are nursing vigorously on her warm milk.

The new kittens do not look much like their parents. You might even wonder if they belong in the same family. For one thing, they are tiny. From nose to tail, they would fit between your elbow and your fingertips. And each only weighs about as much as two big bananas!

But size is not the only difference. The kittens' eyes, when they open, are blue instead of greenish-yellow like their parents'! Their tails are stubby, while their parents' tails are long. Their yellowish-brown coats are covered with dark spots, their parents' coats are a solid color.

Opposite page:

These kittens will lose their spots when they are about six months old.

Tender Mother

The kittens grow quickly on their mother's rich milk. In two weeks their eyes are open, and soon they are tumbling about. After a while, their mother brings them meat from her own catches. Soon they are eating only meat.

The mother cougar stays with her kittens most of the time. She purrs happily as she watches them play and eat. But if they get too rough-and-tumble, she will separate them, grabbing them by the scruff of the neck.

Meat-eaters such as bears—and even male cougars—will hunt the kittens while they are small—that is, if they get a chance. Before letting the kittens leave the den, their mother checks outside for enemies. She sniffs the air, looks around, and gives a low call to the kittens if it is safe to come out. A special "head for safety!" call warns them of danger.

From time to time the mother has to leave her kittens to hunt. Even then she stays nearby. Any animal that comes too close to the den will have to face a fierce and angry mother.

The Basics

Just like young children everywhere, the cougar kittens must learn how to keep themselves clean and neat and how to fend for themselves. Cleanliness is a must, and sharp claws are essential.

Cougars are very careful to keep their long curved claws well sharpened.

Cougars wash themselves just as housecats do. With their long, rough tongues, they lick all the dust and scraps of food from their fur. And they use a front paw, carefully licked between each wash, to clean their faces and behind their ears.

What does a cougar do when its claws get dull? Sharpen them, of course. When your nails get too long, you clip them off. A cougar's claws grow in layers from the inside out, rather like an onion. When the outside layer grows dull, the cat pulls it off by scratching on a tree. That is what your house cat is doing when she scratches on some bark, or the furniture!

This kitten has just learned it doesn't take much skill to stalk a desert tortoise.

Learning the Ropes

To cougar kittens, part of learning how to fend for themselves is learning how to move quietly. When they first move around, they are always stumbling over their own big feet. But with time and practice, they become as strong and agile as acrobats and as quiet as shadows. They can trot through the woods for hours without making a sound. They can climb trees and move among the branches with ease. They can spring from the ground to a tree branch or leap a small stream. They can even swim—and swim well—if they have to.

This cougar kitten sure thinks it's the "cat's meow"!

Practice Makes Purr-fect

Cougar kittens are not born knowing how to hunt. They begin by playing—chasing their mother's tail, pouncing on stray leaves, springing out at one another.

Slowly their mother trains them in the skills they will need. When she brings home meat, she teaches them to attack it before eating. When they are big enough to leave the den, she shows them how to stalk a rabbit and how to catch a porcupine without getting a pawful of quills.

When they are half-grown, she takes them with her one at a time to hunt deer. They learn to catch animals bigger than they are, to pick out weak animals that will not kick at them with sharp hoofs and to keep trying until they make a catch.

Then they must practice—and it takes a lot of practice to become a good hunter!

Cougars are expert climbers of both mountains and trees.

Life Goes On

When the young cougars are about two years old, their mother suddenly becomes grouchy. She will not share her catches, and when they try to play, she loses her temper and cuffs them with her paw. It is time for the mother cougar to start a new family, and she is letting the young cougars know that it is time for them to begin life on their own.

They are ready. They are almost as big as their mother. They are strong, agile and silent. And, although they will not be expert hunters for some time yet, they can hunt well enough to feed themselves.

And so each young cougar sets out to find a territory for itself. It cannot take just any land it likes. It must find a home range where no other cougar is living or where there is a cougar so old or weak that it can easily be driven away.

There the young cougar will live and hunt alone. In time it will mate and new kittens will be born. Eventually they too will take their place in the world . . . and so life goes on.

Words to Know

Den   Animal home.

Guard hairs   Long coarse hairs that make up the outer layer of the cougar's coat.

Litter   Young animals born together.

Mate   To come together to produce young

Nurse   To drink milk from the mother's body.

Paw   The clawed foot of an animal.

Predator   An animal that hunts other animals for food.

Prey   Animal that other animals hunt for food.

Scrapes   Piles of leaves, urine and droppings used to mark the boundaries of a territory.

Territory   Area that an animal or group of animals lives in and often defends from other animals of the same kind.

Zoologist   Scientist who studies animals.

INDEX

Photo Credits: Tim Fitzharris (First Light Associated Photographers), page 4;
Stephen J. Krasemann (Valan Photos), pages 7, 8, 11, 12, 20, 22, 25, 26, 33, 34,
37, 38, 41, 44; Tom W. Hall (Miller Services), pages 15, 16, 43; Hälle Flygare
(Valan Photos), pages 19, 28; Gerhard Kahrmann (Valan Photos), pages 30-31;
Thomas Kitchin (Valan Photos), page 46.

Printed and Bound in Italy by Lego SpA